KU-244-445

INSTRUMENTS *in* MUSIC

WORLD MUSIC

Roger Thomas

Heinemann LIBRARY

First published in Great Britain by Heinemann Library
Halley Court, Jordan Hill, Oxford OX2 8EJ
a division of Reed Educational and Professional Publishing Ltd.
Heinemann is a registered trademark of Reed Educational and Professional Publishing Ltd.

OXFORD FLORENCE PRAGUE MADRID ATHENS
MELBOURNE AUCKLAND KUALA LUMPUR SINGAPORE TOKYO
IBADAN NAIROBI KAMPALA JOHANNESBURG GABORONE
PORTSMOUTH NH (USA) CHICAGO MEXICO CITY SAO PAULO

© Reed Educational and Professional Publishing Ltd 1998

The moral right of the proprietor has been asserted.

All rights reserved. No part of this publication may be reproduced, stored in a retrieval system, or transmitted in any form or by any means, electronic, mechanical, photocopying, recording or otherwise without either the prior written permission of the Publishers or a licence permitting restricted copying in the United Kingdom issued by the Copyright Licensing Agency Ltd, 90 Tottenham Court Road, London WIP 9HE

Designed by Susan Clarke
Printed in Hong Kong

02 01 00 99 98
10 9 8 7 6 5 4 3 2 1
ISBN 0 431 08808 X

DUDLEY PUBLIC LIBRARIE
L   43401
707865   SCH
              J785

British Library Cataloguing in Publication Data

Thomas, Roger
   World music. – (Instruments in music)
   1.World music – Juvenile literature 2.Musical Instruments – Juvenile literature
   I.Title
   781.4'163

Acknowledgements
The Publishers would like to thank the following for permission to reproduce photographs:
Gareth Boden, p.26 (Royal Festival Hall Gamelan Department); Robin Broadbank, pp.5 bottom, 15; Trevor Clifford, p.6 left (Hertfordshire County Music Service), p.6 right (Wembley Drum Centre), p.12 left (El Mundo Flamenco); Liz Eddison, pp.12 right, 16, p.14 (Hobgoblin Music); Alf Goodrich, pp.4, 5 top, 24; Chris Howes, pp.8, 9; Hutchison Library, pp.20, 25, p.29 (Sarah Errington), p.2 (J G Fuller), pp.7 (Dirk R. Frans); J. Allan Cash, pp.18, 19; Panos Pictures, p.11 (Penny Tweedie); Pictor Uniphoto, p.27; Redferns, p.21. p.13 (G. Brandon); Tony Stone, p.23 (John Elk), p.10 (Paul Sounders); Trip, p.28 (B. Gibbs); Zefa, p.17

Cover photograph: Redferns/Mick Hutson

Our thanks to Betty Root for her comments in the preparation of this book.

Every effort has been made to contact copyright holders of any material reproduced in this book. Any omissions will be rectified in subsequent printings if notice is given to the Publisher.

CONTENTS

Introduction 4

India: the sitar and the tabla 6

Native America: drums 8

Australia: the didgeridoo and stamping sticks 10

Spain: the flamenco guitar and castanets 12

The Middle East: the oud and darabouka 14

South America: pan-pipes and vihuela 16

Trinidad: steel pans 18

Africa: the sansa and kora 20

Japan: the shakuhachi and koto 22

China: the pi-pa and sheng 24

Indonesia: the gamelan orchestra 26

Singing in world music 28

Glossary 30

Further reading 31

Index 32

Some words are shown in bold, **like this**.
You can find out what they mean by looking
in the Glossary.

INTRODUCTION

This book is about just a very few of the many instruments used in the music of different countries. This is sometimes called 'world music'.

We cannot visit every country where music is made. But we can still find out about the thousands of different instruments played across the world

There are many kinds of instruments in this book. But often they will work in the same way as the instruments of our own country. Today, we can hear world music in concerts and on CDs wherever we live.

INDIA:
THE SITAR AND TABLA

The sitar has many metal strings. The player plucks some of the strings with a **plectrum** attached to one finger and changes the notes by pressing the strings down on **frets** on the **neck** of the instrument. The other strings add to the sound. The strings buzz against a **bridge** when the instrument is played.

tabla

sitar

The sitar and tabla are important instruments in Indian music. They are often played together

This musician is playing the tabla

The tabla is a set of two drums. One plays high notes and is often made of wood. The other has a low pitch and is often made of metal. They are played with the player's hands. The player can change the notes of the low-pitched drum by pressing the **drumhead** as he plays.

NATIVE AMERICA: DRUMS

Drums of different kinds are very important in **traditional** Native American music. The shells of the drums are made of wood. The **drumheads** are made of **hide**. The drums are often decorated. Native American musicians also use rattles, flutes and whistles.

This drum is a Native American drum

This Native American is playing
a traditional drum

Native American drums have a booming sound.
They are often used in **religious ceremonies** when
they are played as people sing. They are also used
when people dance. Native American instruments
are traditionally believed to have magical powers.

AUSTRALIA: THE DIDGERIDOO AND STAMPING STICKS

The didgeridoo is a long wooden trumpet made from a hollow branch. It has a **mouthpiece** made from **beeswax**. The player blows into the mouthpiece so that his lips make a sound into the instrument. The didgeridoo has one main note but the player can change it slightly by blowing harder or softer. It has a deep, growling sound.

This Aboriginal Australian musician is playing a didgeridoo

These Aboriginal Australian dancers are using stamping sticks

Stamping sticks are long wooden sticks which are used as **percussion** instruments. They are played by stamping them on the ground.

SPAIN: THE FLAMENCO GUITAR AND CASTANETS

Flamenco is a type of **traditional** Spanish music which uses instruments, singing and dancing. The flamenco guitar has six strings which the player strums up and down with his or her fingernails. The guitar has two scratchplates to stop the player's nails from scratching the wooden top of the guitar.

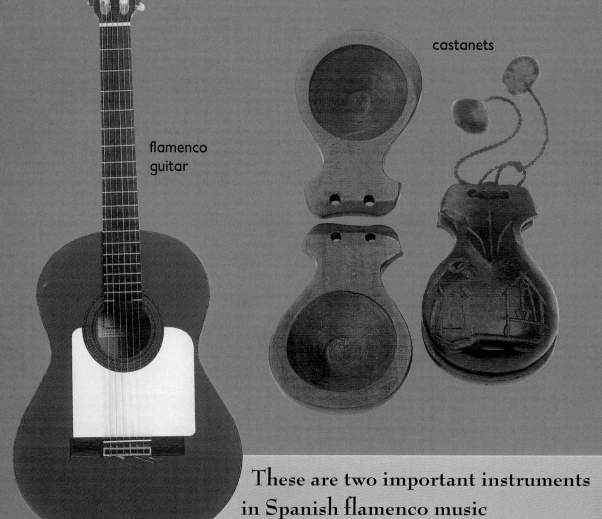

castanets

flamenco guitar

These are two important instruments in Spanish flamenco music

These musicians and dancers are performing flamenco music

Castanets are small wooden **percussion** instruments. They are attached to the dancer's fingers with cords. They make a sharp clicking sound. They are usually played in each hand by flamenco dancers while they dance. The dancer fits the **rhythm** of the castanets to the rhythm of the dance.

THE MIDDLE EAST: THE OUD AND DARABOUKA

The darabouka is a funnel-shaped drum with an opening at one end. It can be made from clay, metal or wood. The player can tap the **drumhead** with his fingers to make a bright, high sound. The player can also slap the drumhead with his hand to make a deep, booming sound.

darabouka

oud

The oud and darabouka are played in many Middle Eastern countries

This Arab musician is playing an oud

The oud is a string instrument with a rounded back. The player plucks and strums the strings with a **plectrum**. The player changes the notes by pressing the strings against the **neck** of the instrument. The oud has a softer sound than a guitar because the neck has no metal **frets**.

SOUTH AMERICA: PAN-PIPES AND VIHUELA

The vihuela is like a small guitar. The instrument was invented in Spain. It was made of wood. It became used in South American music because Spanish people went to South America five hundred years ago. South American people sometimes use an **armadillo** shell to make the body of the instrument instead of wood.

These are two **traditional** South American instruments

pan-pipes

vihuela

This South American musician is playing the pan-pipes

The pan-pipes are a set of wooden tubes. They are played in the Andes region of South America where they are called 'yupana'. They make a sound when the player blows across the ends of the tubes. The pan-pipes have a soft, breathy sound.

TRINIDAD: STEEL PANS

People all over the world enjoy steel pan music from Trinidad. The pans have a soft, ringing sound. Some steel pans are now made in factories but they were first made from old steel barrels. The people making them hammer dents into the top of the barrel from underneath. Then the barrel is heated to make the steel very hard.

This is how a full orchestra of steel pans is set up

These musicians from the West Indies are playing steel pans and other **percussion** instruments

Steel pans have different names depending on how many notes they can play and whether the notes are low or high. Some of the names are borrowed from other instruments. The names are: rhythm, ping pong, second pan, cello, guitar and bass.

AFRICA: THE SANSA AND KORA

The sansa is made like a wooden box. A set of metal or **cane** strips is fixed tightly to the box. The player plucks them with his thumbs or fingers to make the notes. Long strips make low notes and short strips make high notes. The sansa makes a sharp, twangy sound.

The sansa is played in many African countries

The kora is played in Gambia, which is a country in Africa

The kora has 21 strings and a long wooden **neck**. The neck is fixed to a big hollowed-out dried vegetable called a gourd. A large hole in the gourd is covered with a tight animal skin. The player plucks the strings with his fingers and thumbs. The kora is often played when people sing. It has a soft but lively sound.

JAPAN: THE SHAKUHACHI AND KOTO

The shakuhachi is a flute made from **bamboo**. The bamboo is chosen and cut very carefully to get a good sound. The player blows across the end of the shakuhachi to make the sound and covers holes on the instrument with his fingers to change the notes. The shakuhachi has a clear, pure sound.

This shakuhachi player is wearing a **traditional** head-dress

22

These Japanese musicians are playing kotos

The koto is a large instrument with 13 **silk** or **nylon** strings. The player has three **plectra** on the fingers of one hand and uses them to pluck the strings. Each string is stretched over a **bridge**. The player can press the strings on the other side of the bridge with the other hand while playing. This gives the notes a bendy sound.

CHINA: THE PI-PA AND SHENG

The pi-pa has been played in China for about 2000 years. It is made of wood and has four **silk** strings which the player plucks. The player changes the notes by pressing the strings against wooden **frets** on the body and **neck** of the instrument. It has a soft but clear sound.

This Chinese musician is playing a pi-pa

The sheng is a bundle of tubes with reeds inside them

To play the sheng, the player blows into the tubes through a **mouthpiece**. To make the notes the player covers holes on the tubes with his or her fingers. This lets the air reach the **reeds** to make them sound. To stop a note, the player uncovers the hole and the air escapes before reaching the reed.

INDONESIA: THE GAMELAN ORCHESTRA

The gamelan orchestra is a mixture of **tuned percussion** instruments, drums and **gongs**. The lead musician will sometimes play a **fiddle** or flute. There are lots of sizes of gamelan orchestra, made up from different numbers of these instruments.

The gamelan orchestra has many different instruments

Playing gamelan music

The instruments of the gamelan orchestra are played with mallets. The metal instruments make a soft, bell-like sound. The drums are played with the hands and help with the **rhythm** of the music.

SINGING IN WORLD MUSIC

People of all ages love to sing. Singing is a part of nearly every kind of world music. Singers from different parts of the world will use their voices in quite different ways. People can sing alone or in groups.

This is a group of Indian singers

This is a Chinese opera singer

Singing is used in religious worship in many countries. Songs can also tell stories, give advice or describe how the singer is feeling. Singing can also be just for fun!

GLOSSARY

armadillo a small animal with a bony shell

bamboo a plant which grows into strong hollow stalks

beeswax a substance made by bees in beehives. When it is warmed it can be moulded into different shapes like clay

bridge a part of a stringed instrument with a thin edge over which the strings are stretched

cane a piece of bamboo or a piece from a similar hard, woody plant

drumhead the flat surface of a drum which the drummer plays on. It can be made of animal skin

fiddle another name for a violin. The name is sometimes used for other violin-like instruments

frets thin metal rods on the neck of a stringed instrument which the strings are pressed onto to change the notes

gongs flat metal percussion instruments which are usually round in shape. A gong is played with a beater. It makes a note with a crashing, hissing sound

hide dried animal skin

mouthpiece the part of a wind instrument which the player blows into

neck a long piece of wood on a stringed instrument which the strings are stretched along

nylon a very strong type of plastic which can be made into strings for musical instruments

percussion instruments which are played by tapping or hitting

plectrum a flat piece of wood or plastic used for plucking the strings on a stringed instrument. The word for more than one plectrum is **plectra**

reeds thin strips of cane or metal which make a sound when air is blown across them

religious ceremonies special acts of worship which may involve many people

rhythm the regular pattern of notes in music

silk a very strong thread which is made by a kind of moth

traditional any kind of music which has been played for a long time in the history of a country

tuned percussion percussion instruments which can play many notes

FURTHER READING

Live Music! Elizabeth Sharma. Wayland, 1992

You may need help to read these other titles on music.

Eyewitness Kit: Music. Dorling Kindersley, 1993

How the World Makes Music. Iwo Zaluski and Pamela Zaluski. Young Library, 1994

The World of Music: With CD. Nicola Barber and Mary Mure. Evans Brothers, 1994

INDEX

castanets 12, 13

CDs 5

Chinese opera 29

concerts 5

darabouka 14

didgeridoo 10

drum 6, 7, 8, 9, 14, 26, 27

fiddle 26

flamenco guitar 12

flute 8, 26

gamelan 26, 27

gong 26

kora 21

koto 23

oud 14, 15

pan-pipes 16, 17

pi-pa 24

rattles 8

sansa 20

shakuhachi 22

sheng 25

singing 28, 29

sitar 6

stamping sticks 11

steel pans 18, 19

tabla 6, 7

vihuela 16

voice 28, 29

whistles 8

yupana 17